Weapons

Secrets of the

Knife

Volume 1 - Empty Hand

David Seiwert

DISCLAIMER

Please note that the publisher, the author, or anyone appearing in this instructional book is Not Responsible in any manner whatsoever for any injury which may occur by reading and/or following the instructions herein. When training you should wear safety glasses and ALWAYS use a practice training knife. At no time should a 'live' (sharp) knife or blade be used in your training.

This book is for informational purposes only. This book is not meant to be used as a training guide without the guidance of a qualified instructor.

It is essential that before following any of the activities, physical or otherwise, herein described, the reader or readers should first consult his or her physician for advice on whether or not the reader or readers should embark on the physical activity described herein. Since the physical activities described herein may be too sophisticated in nature, it is essential that a physician be consulted.

It is also advised to check with your local law enforcement for guidance on self-defense. Use the minimal force necessary to overcome an attacker.

Dear Reader,

Thanks for purchasing *"Secrets of the Knife" - Vol. 1*, and I hope that you will enjoy it.

As an Independent author I don't have a big marketing department or the exposure of being on bookshelves in the mall.

If you enjoy this book please help spread the work by telling your friends and leaving me a review on Amazon. Reviews are what helps the book to get noticed. The more reviews that I have the more it will help to get acknowledged in the search engines.

I appreciate your support by the purchase of this book. You are making it possible for me to continue to produce many more products such as this.

David Seiwert

David Seiwert on Amazon, **http://amzn.to/2mXsgEE**

ACKNOWLEDGMENTS

I would like to thank the following individuals, for without their contributions and support this book would not have been written:

Joe Hinnenkamp, Dave Thompson, Don Wong for their help demonstrating the techniques.

My wife Thana for her great photography work

Thanks to my Beta readers Bill Hartmann and Bill Steelman.

Other books by the author:

*"**KunTao** - The esoteric martial art of Southeast Asia"*

*"Secrets of the **Karambit"***

Available at our website or on Amazon

http://amzn.to/2mXsgEE

http://dfamediaproductions.com/books.html

Watch for "Secrets of the Knife - Volume 2" coming soon
This book will deal with Knife vs. Knife

Cover design by DFA Media Productions

Published by DFA Media Productions

Contents

To view video clips of some of the following drills and techniques go to:

http://bit.ly/2mFZPJJ

Preface

The EDC (every day carry) knife has been extremely popular for centuries, and there is a wide variety of books, videos and information available. So why write another one?

A number of reasons:

It is difficult to find a comprehensive book on knife training and defensive moves outside of military manuals and a few martial arts books. Most simply show you techniques, but never go into drills or concepts. Techniques are fine, but you need to be able to adapt to an ever changing situation. No two attackers or situations are ever the same, everyone reacts differently in a hostile environment and you need to be prepared.

While there is some information about the Southeast Asian martial arts such as Silat, KunTao and the Filipino arts of Kali and Escrima, they are grossly underrepresented and all but unknown to the general public.

It is my hope that this book will help everyone interested in learning more about the Southeast Asian Arts and their unique approach to using the knife both defensively and offensively.

David Seiwert

Notes

Prologue

In present-day culture many people will suggest that there is no need to learn knife avoidance, knife self-defense or knife 'fighting'. They think that if they are ever confronted with an armed attacker they will just comply with the demands and that will be the end of it. Perhaps they are correct, perhaps not.

In the latest figures available by the FBI there were:
1567 murders committed using a blade
23,680 robberies at knife point, and
126,187 assaults with knives

In Europe we see something similar, according to The Daily Mail in the UK there were over 130,000 knife attacks last year.

The percentage of knife attacks in the USA is around 13% while in Europe it is closer to 43%. In recent years there has been an increase of attacks in China and throughout Asia as well as in the Middle East.

Knife assaults can be extremely dangerous and it is best to avoid them if you can, but sometimes that is not possible. Carrying a firearm can help to equalize the situation, but it is not a panacea to the problem. If you cannot get to the weapon then it does you no good and at close range a knife usually has the edge (no pun intended).

All that I am suggesting is to become familiar with the weapon. I am not saying that by reading this book you will become impervious to attacks, but it is a good idea to become familiar with them and other weapons in order to de-mystify and take some of the fear away. If you understand how it can be used for an attack then you can begin to understand how to apply a suitable defense.

Notes

Part 1 - Basics

Notes

Chapter 1 - History of the Arts

The drills, concepts, and techniques found in this book are predominately from Southeast Asia, specifically the Indonesian art of Silat, the art of Kuntao (kuntaw) and the Filipino Martial Arts such as Kali, Escrima and Arnis.

Silat, Kuntao and FMA are generic terms and within these arts you can find hundreds of different styles. Most of these systems are passed down between family members or among peoples from a certain village, tribe or region.

Filipino Martial Arts
When many people think of FMA they think of stick fighting, but the Filipino arts are much much more and are world renowned for their blade culture. Knives, bolos (machete) and swords have been in play for centuries in the Philippines and they have brought the art to an unparalleled skill level.

Knives and blades are used on a daily basis from the farmer in the fields to the coconut vendor in the market. There are over 7,000 islands in the Philippines and many villages, towns and rural areas. Even if you go to a big city like Manila you can still see people in the outdoor markets who are adept with a knife because they use it on daily basis.

I have a student from the Philippines who once told me that when he was young (5 or 6 yrs old) it was his 'job' to loosen up his father's new balisong knives. It seems that when they are new they are a bit stiff to open and his task was to continually flip the blades open and closed for hours on end until they moved freely.

Filipino martial arts are considered one of the most advanced, practical and deadly blade arts in the world. Military and law enforcement agencies worldwide have adopted many of their training methods.

In fact weapons are generally taught first in FMA unlike most martial arts which start their training with punches and kicks. The weapon (generally the short stick) is seen to be an extension of the hand and is used interchangeably. This is why FMA practitioners' are so adept with weapons, they start working with them early on and continue working with weapons throughout their training.

When working with the blade there are three things to keep in mind; fluidity, rhythm and timing, all key elements in Southeast Asian arts. The blade is a 'live' and fluid weapon not static.

The movements are fast, unpredictable and constantly shifting, you need to be able to reciprocate in the same manner, learning to flow and to quickly responding to your opponents changing attacks are probably the most difficult things for people to learn and apply.

Indonesian Martial Arts

Silat is a generic term for the indigenous martial arts of the Indonesian and Malay Archipelago and the entire region of the Malay Peninsula. Silat is practiced throughout Indonesia, Malaysia, Singapore, Brunei, southern Thailand, Vietnam and the southern Philippines.

Silat has been practiced since at least the 6th century and has influences from India and China. Images shown in the Hindu and Buddhist texts of Ramayana show the Indian influence on Silat weapons. Djurus (forms or katas) are said to have been introduced by the monk Bodhidharma.

Silat is well known for its use of weapons, especially the blade. It is often said that 'Without the knife there is no Silat'. Students of the art will learn many bladed weapons, such as the sword and the straight blade as well as the curved knife known as the karambit. The art of Silat is probably best known for the kris, a wavy blade shaped like a flame or serpents tongue.

Unlike the Filipino arts, most Silat systems teach empty hand techniques first and the weapons later. Much of the weapons training is also taught in choreographed routines (similar to forms or katas) called Djuros or Langkahs, something that the majority of FMA styles do not have.

There are hundreds of Silat systems taught throughout the world, some of them are more traditional and strictly taught for fighting while others have been modified in order to be used in tournament competition. Many of the silat systems as practiced by the Chinese in Southeast Asia may be referred to as KunTao or KunTao-Silat.

KunTao
KunTao is also a generic term used by people throughout Southeast Asia (Indonesia, Malaysia, Brunei, coastal Thailand, the Philippines, Cambodia and Vietnam) to describe the martial arts fighting methods brought to the region by the Hakka people of southern China.

As the Hakka people migrated south through China, the arts that they brought with them were then modified and blended with the southern styles into the Hakka kuen systems in the Fujian, Jiangxi, and Guangdong regions of southern China.

There are currently over 100 systems of KunTao, and every style looks different depending on the country of origin and what animal or style/system that it is patterned after. The relationship between KunTao and the indigenous martial arts found in Indonesia, Malaysia, Thailand and the western Philippines (spelled kuntaw and sometimes called Filipino kung fu) is not entirely clear.

Modern KunTao has been blended with arts from the countries of Southeast Asia, with many of the more popular systems come from Indonesia, Malaysia and Brunei and have a distinct silat influence.

You can read more in the book "KunTao: The Esoteric Martial Art of Southeast Asia."

Chapter 2 - Types of Grips

Forward Grip

There are 2 basic ways to hold the knife, a forward grip and a reverse grip. The forward grip is also referred to as the 'Hammer Grip' and the reverse is typically called the 'Icepick Grip'. With the forward grip, the fingers are wrapped tightly around the handle with the thumb touching the forefinger and middle finger, very much like making a fist. The edge of the blade is facing outward and in line with the second set of knuckles (phalanges) of the fingers. This is the most common way to brandish a knife.

This grip feels the most comfortable for most people and it is the way that we hold most tools such as a hammer, screwdriver, wrench, or others. The main advantage is the extended reach that it allows and it can be used in a stabbing or slashing motion.

However, when the knife is being held in the forward grip, the hand is usually extended which can make it (the hand) vulnerable to a counter attack by being slashed or grabbed. The further away from your body that you try to apply your attack the less force that you are able to generate due to the fact that you need to tilt the hand and wrist forward in order to maintain contact with the target, although this is not a huge problem since we are talking about an edged weapon.

The weakness with this grip is an attack from the rear. It is extremely difficult to mount a successful counter to an aggressor moving in from behind without turning 90-180 degrees to meet the incoming assault.

Forward Grip: Saber Position

This is a variation of the forward grip where you place your thumb on top of the spine of the blade or the thumb rise on the handle. With this grip, you can apply pressure with the thumb allowing you to tilt the blade forward at a 45 deg. as opposed to the 90 deg angle when held in the traditional forward grip. This will not only extend your reach, but allows for better control of the blade.

The disadvantage is that it is not as secure as the forward grip because the thumb does not wrap around the handle, but is facing forward on the thumb rise. This causes a gap or opening between the thumb and forefinger which could allow for a disarm of the knife or the blade being stripped from your hand if a tight and secure grip is not maintained.

If you wanted to deploy a fixed blade in a forward grip, then a cross draw (reaching with your right hand to the left side) or having the sheath secured behind your back may be the way to go.

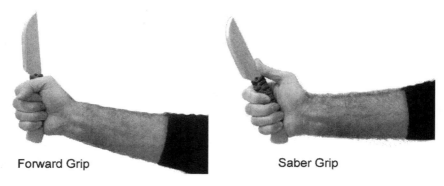

Forward Grip   Saber Grip

Reverse Grip: Edge Out
The reverse grip or icepick grip is used for close range work since you do not have the same reach as you do when using the forward grip. The reversed grip is primarily used for slashing techniques (with the edge facing outward) although tremendous force can be generated when driving it in a downward vertical angle.

The blade can be held with the thumb covering the fingers as if making a fist or you can place the thumb on the butt of the knife handle thereby 'capping' the knife and increasing the force and security of the grip.

For a fixed blade this would be a common way to deploy the blade especially when in close or if you are knocked to the ground.

A drawback is the lack of penetration with this grip. The majority of the attacks will be slashing attacks unless you strike in a vertical or backhanded motion. This isn't all bad, but slashing attacks will take longer to dispatch an attacker than thrusting moves which have more penetration and therefore do more damage.

Reverse Grip: Edge In
The reverse grip has the edge of the blade facing inward towards the user and is used in a raking or clawing fashion. It is good for stabbing as tremendous force can be brought down on the point of the blade. This grip can also be used to hook the opponent's arm or limb and pull him into you.

On the minus side, it is never really a good idea to be cutting towards yourself with a blade. If your blade gets trapped against your body or you fall on the blade it could be a problem.

Reverse Grip - Edge Out

Reverse Grip - Edge In

Defanging the Snake

One phrase that you commonly hear in Southeast Asian arts is 'Defanging the Snake". This refers to the tactic of stripping the weapon from the attacker's hand, be it a knife, gun, ball bat or another type of implement. The theory is that if you can 'defang' or remove the threat then you have a better chance at surviving.

Now this can also involve 'destroying' or breaking a limb (arm, leg), tearing a ligament, muscle or other similar damage. If you can cause injury to the assailant's appendage you get the same effect, if they can't stand up then they can't continue the fight or assault, if you break the hand then they cannot hold a fighting implement, but it usually implies disarming the weapon, generally a knife.

In order to defang the snake when using a knife, you would simply cut his fingers, hand or wrist in order to cause the attacker to drop his weapon. When you don't have a weapon of your own then damaging the limb is not as easy to do.

In order to have any chance at disarming your opponent there are a few things that you need to be aware of:

- **Do not chase the blade!** - You never go into a situation like this with the intent of doing a disarm.

- **Disarms can be accidental or incidental!** - During an attack a disarm will just happen to be there as a consequence or your counter moves. Do not go looking for it or you will be cut, but if an opportunity presents itself then take it.

- **You must do damage!** - Being able to disarm a weapon requires that you do damage to the person wielding the weapon. If you simply try to grab the weapon without first hurting the attacker it will be extremely difficult if not impossible. Without first causing damage such as a strike to the hand, kick to the shin or fingers to the eye, all of his energy and strength will be focused on maintaining control of the weapon.

- **The main threat is the attacker, not the weapon!** - In order to have any hope of coming out of the situation alive, you need to do as much damage to the attacker as you can. Once you put him out of commission the knife is no longer a threat.

Notes

Chapter 3 - Angles of Attack

Now these angles will vary from system to system, but what we are showing you here are the strikes that we use and you will see that they cover every possible striking direction.

The Angles

Angles #1 and #2 are diagonal down strikes, these slash downward from the shoulder to the waist, usually......what most people don't understand or realize is that an angle #1 can be ANY diagonal down strike.

Angle #1

It can go from the shoulder to the waist, from the waist to the knee or knee to the ankle, the height does not matter, what matters is the direction of the strike.

Angle #2 *goes from left to right*

Angles #3 and #4 are horizontal strikes, typically across the midsection but again, it can be any height. An angle #3 can slash across the eyes, the face, the neck, the midsection or....well, you get the point as long as it is horizontal it is an angle #3 or #4.

Angle #3

Angle #4

Angle #5 is a straight thrusting attack typically to the mid-section.

Angle #5

Angles #6 (from left to right) and #7 (from right to left) are diagonal up strikes from the knee to the waist or from the waist to the shoulder.

Angle #6

Angle #7

Angles #8 and #9 are vertical strikes, angle #8 is a vertical down from the head to the groin and #9 is a vertical up, from the groin to the head.

Angle #8

Angle #9

These nine attacking angles can be done with the forward (hammer) grip or the reverse (ice pick) grip.

Next we'll take a look at the strikes on the B.O.B. (body opponent bag) dummy.

Angle #8

Angle #9

In case you are wondering why the striking angles are being shown in a book about knife defense the answer is simple, in order to be able to defend against something you need to know how to use it offensively.

Notes

Chapter 4 - Stances

Being successful during a knife attack requires you to not only have good defensive skills, but you must also maintain awareness and be aggressive with the execution of your offensive techniques and counters. In order to stay alive during a knife encounter, you must counter-attack as forceful and violently as you are able. At the same time, it is extremely important to protect your vital organs along with the face, throat, wrists and major arteries. So you must use caution when countering and not move in with reckless abandon.

While this may sound like a contradiction in terms, it is vital when your life is on the line. You cannot passively execute your blocks or counters against a live blade and hope to survive. The knife needs very little pressure to cut flesh, it only needs to touch or slash your skin to cause damage, so you need to attack as aggressively as you can.

A knife attack is 'live' or fluid not static, the blade is constantly moving, and if you block an attack from one angle the attacker will simply go around or redirect his strike. You must hurt, injure and disable the attacker if you have any hope of coming out of the situation alive.

Although this book deals with empty hand methods against the knife we will also show stances used when holding the knife so that you know what to look for and how to deal with it.

There are three basic stances that can be used when employing the blade, right lead, left lead a neutral stance along with a few variations.

Assuming that you are right-handed (80% of the population uses the right hand) when using the right lead the right hand and right foot are forward and closer to the attacker.

Right Side Forward

Left Side Forward

In the left lead, the left leg is forward with the right hand (the one holding the blade) to the rear and the left hand is held in front of the body to protect you from a counter-attack. The left hand can also be used in an offensive manner to off-balance the opponent. Some systems refer to the left hand as the 'sacrifice hand' when used in this manner.

There are pros and cons to both and you will rarely get two people to agree on which is better. The thing to do is practice both stances in many different scenarios and decide which is best for you.

Now looking at a few variations, you can use the knife in a forward or reverse grip and you can also keep the knife hidden behind the right thigh in a hammer grip or palmed (running along the forearm) using the icepick grip.

So you technically have six different ways to use the knife, but only three stances.

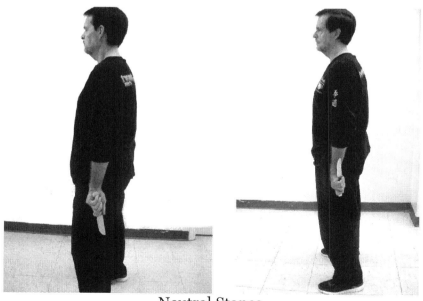

Neutral Stance

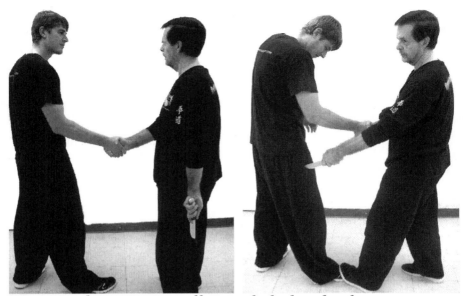

Be wary when someone offers to shake hands after an argument. Notice how I step on his foot to keep him from moving away until I complete my attack.

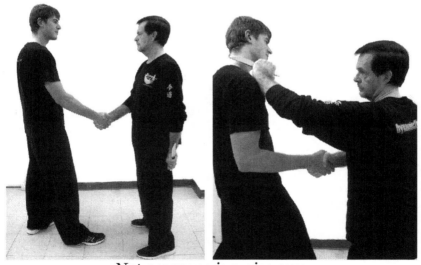

Not everyone is a nice guy.

Looking at the empty hand stance you pretty much have the same three stances to choose from, right lead, left lead and a square stance (your feet are more or less parallel).

Regardless of which stance you choose your hands must be in an upward position to protect the body. You should naturally move to this position (with the hands up) as if to say 'Take it easy, I don't want any trouble'. This way, if and when an attack does come your arms are already in the correct position to block or counter an incoming strike while only having to move your arms a few inches.

By contrast, if you leave your arms at your sides when the attack comes there is no way that you can get your hands up to your head fast enough to stop the assault.

You will also want to have your palms facing towards you (if there is a weapon) in the event of a slashing attack by your assailant. If your palms are facing outward towards the attacker you can have a major problem. The inside of the forearms contain the tendons, blood vessels and arteries, if these are severed your chances for survival have been significantly diminished.

Your weight should be evenly distributed while the rear leg is up on the ball of the foot for quick mobility. The knees are slightly bent and the elbows are in at the sides with the hands up for protection. Keep the chin tucked in to protect the throat. You need to be able to be mobile, movement is imperative during a knife attack.

Right Side Forward

Left Side Forward

    If you have a jacket or sweatshirt on you should immediately remove it and wrap it around the arm that is held in front for some protection from the blade, the hand in front is usually called the 'sacrifice or live hand'. If you have a purse, backpack, briefcase or something similar you can hold it in front of you as a shield.

    If two people are unarmed then they are evenly matched (more or less), but if you add a weapon any weapon into the mix suddenly the scales are tipped in favor of the person holding the weapon.

Regardless of your skill or knowledge, you should never attempt to go against a knife wielding attacker if you are unarmed unless you have no other choice. Your first option should always be to run to safety. If running is not an option, then hopefully some knowledge will help you to live through the encounter.

In a situation like this fear is your biggest enemy and overcoming it can mean the difference between life and death. Some fear is good as it keeps you alert and heightens the senses, but too much can be a hindrance and immobilize you.

One sure way to help to overcome fear is through practice and training, this will allow you to react instead of over-thinking the situation.

There are entire books written on dealing with and overcoming fear and are not able to be dealt with within the confines of this book however.

Chapter 5 - Footwork

Footwork is essential when using or facing a bladed weapon. Using good footwork in conjunction with your blocking will help you to avoid the weapon much better than just blocking alone and separates the high-caliber warrior from the average warrior.

There are many types of footwork methods and many ways to train them. The three most common are: linear, angular and circular. All three types can be used for offensive and defensive movements and all three have their advantages and disadvantages in any given situation which is why they are usually used together.

Linear footwork

Linear footwork is simply moving in a straight line backward and forward or side to side, either by shuffling or stepping as in a walking fashion.

Moving backward is ok to evade the initial attack, but sooner or later you will run out of space if you keep retreating. In addition, by only moving in a straight line you are still in the 'line of fire' of the attack whether it is a gun, knife or fist. Moving to the side may be a better option depending on the situation as now you are 'offline' or out of the way of the attack.

If you move back to evade and then quickly move in to stop the aggressor (while keeping the weapon at bay), you will stand a better chance at surviving. In order to counter attack, you must close the gap.

Remember: *the knife, gun, pipe or hammer by itself cannot harm you; it is the person holding it who is the problem and must be stopped at all costs. This can only be done by getting inside of his weapons range using footwork.*

Angular or triangle footwork

Angular or triangle footwork is a more advanced way of stepping and is extremely effective against an opponent with a weapon.

Angular stepping allows you to move offline and away from the trajectory of the weapon as well as provide an opportunity for closing the distance gap between you and the attacker.

Forward Angle: *Notice that the legs are bent and that you are not locking into a stance as you would in traditional martial*

arts. Your footwork must be fluid and flowing. This stepping allows you to move into your opponent.

Reverse Angle: *With this, you move away from the attack, you can use your arms to help to guide the attack past you if you choose.*

Circular stepping

Circular stepping is another evasive stepping tactic that is difficult to employ, but if you can master the maneuver it can be very effective in countering your opponents attack by allowing you to move into his blind spot which, by the time he figures out where you have gone, it is too late.

Circular Stepping*: Starting with either foot is fine. Starting with the left foot (as shown) takes you out on a wider perimeter around your opponent while starting with the right foot would allow you to stay in closer to him.*

Here are a few examples:

Technique 1

Technique #1 *- Player 'B' attacks with an angle #1 while Player 'A' parries the blade away from him while grabbing the arm and attacking with a finger jab to the eyes and finishing with an elbow to the face. Player 'A' is using Angular and then Linear footwork to close the gap between him and the attacker.*

As you will notice throughout this book it is best to stay outside of the attacking arm if you can. Moving inside of his arms gives him a greater opportunity for more strikes. Notice also that after the Forward Angle 'A' uses a Linear step to shuffle forward to reach his target. Very often the steps are used in conjunction with each other.

Technique 2

Technique #2 - 'B' attacks with an angle #3 (horizontal strike) while 'A' steps back and hollows out his mid-section while blocking downward (following the force). These moves should be executed at the same time. Then shuffling forward (Linear step) 'A' locks up the arm while striking the face. Player 'A' could then finish with a takedown.

Technique 3

Technique #3 - 'B' attacks with an angle #8 as 'A' parries, blocks and strikes to the eyes.

From here 'A' shuffles in while striking the chin (notice how he still controls the arm)

Using circular stepping he works his way behind the opponent and finishes with a choke.

Now one type of stepping is not necessarily better than another and most of the time they are used in combination with each other.

When attacking with the blade or defending against the knife you will find that footwork is an indispensable component to have in your arsenal. Remember, with a knife it only takes a 'touch' to do tremendous damage.

So it is imperative that your body is in constant motion, moving from long to middle to close range and out again in order to avoid his attack or to mount a counterattack of your own, footwork is what will allow you to do this.

The mobility of the hands and feet are vital to surviving a knife encounter and they must work together to maximize your ability to attack and defend, the more that you move the less of a target you present to your enemy.

Now, these are only a few of the dozens of variations of footwork maneuvers available in Southeast Asian arts, in fact, I could write the entire book about footwork alone.

Notes

Chapter 6 - Ranges

Ranges

When involved in a knife encounter it is also vital to maintain the proper distance to avoid being cut.

Combat consists of four ranges, and it's important that you become proficient in all of them. The ability to maneuver in and out of each range with control and agility is just one of the many skills needed for success during a conflict or assault.

In doing research for this book I have found that there are many schools of thought on this subject, alternating from three ranges all the way up to eight different ranges.

To simplify things I personally teach four fighting ranges, the ranges are based on the most logical tools (hands or feet) or tactics being used. The ranges are as follows:

Long Range - At this distance you are far enough away from the attacker that he cannot reach you with his blade during an attack. This range is for avoidance of the weapon, but you may be able to apply a kick (to the low line only) at this range. The knife is usually in the forward grip.

Middle Range - At this range you can make contact with the assailants arm or body, but be aware that he can also reach you.

Close or CQC (Close Quarter Combative) Range - At close range you are close enough to strike with elbows, head butts or grab with your hands. Holding the knife in the reverse grip can be very effective in this range.

Ground or Grappling Range - Obviously this is the most dangerous range to be in when a weapon is involved. It is imperative that you disarm, disable or escape before things get to this point.

Ranges

Ground or Grappling Range

As you train, study and practice, it's important that you identify and strengthen your strongest fighting range and also your weakest range. Most of us like to take the path of least resistance, meaning that if there is a range or a skill that we are weak in we tend to ignore it or try to justify why we don't need to be concerned with our weakness.

If you are honest with yourself, you will admit where your abilities are deficient and take a course, read a book or watch videos to improve your skills in the area where you are lacking.

The key component for staying safe during a knife assault is distance. Many people will tell you that they are not worried about an attacker because they carry a firearm. Well, I'm here to tell you that a street attack doesn't happen like a gunfight in an old western movie. The attack will be quick and personal. If you don't know how to deal with it while unarmed you may never have a chance to get to your weapon.

Most people don't know of the "21 foot Rule" and even fewer have heard of it called the Tueller Drill. The Tueller Drill was devised by Sergeant Dennis Tueller of the Salt Lake City, Utah police department way back in 1983.

The drill was a self-defense training exercise to determine the minimum distance that a police officer could safely allow between himself and an attacker, before it was too late to be able to brandish his own weapon. After testing the drill at different distances it was determined that 21 feet is the MINIMUM distance that can safely be allowed.
How can that be?

The drill works like this: The 2 trainees face each other at a distance of 20 feet apart while the person with the gun has it holstered (remember he's the good guy) and the knife is already in the bad guys hand.

Tueller Drill   1   2

20 ft covered
in 1.5 seconds

3

4

At a predetermined signal the attacker runs full speed at the potential victim. The shooter must draw his weapon and shoot the attacker without backing up (if he backs up, he is adding distance and it is no longer 20 feet).

It was found that the attacker could travel the distance of 20 feet in 1.5 seconds! At 20 feet the shooter was able to draw and fire the weapon hitting the attacker just as he reached and stabbed the shooter. At any distance closer than 20 ft. the man with the knife was ALWAYS able to stab the shooter before he could be shot.

That's how the determination of 21 feet was established as the minimum amount of distance for safety.

Now I tell this story not to say that guns are ineffective, but to demonstrate how dangerous and effective a knife can be. If you carry a knife, gun or any weapon...........know how to use it.

Part 2 - Training

Click on or go to the link below to view the videos of the Drills and Techniques shown in this book to see how they are done.

http://bit.ly/2mFZPJJ

Chapter 7 - Blocking

Blocking

Obviously, the best way to block the knife is not to be in the path of its carnage, but this may not be possible in all cases. As mentioned in the chapter on 'Stances', if you have a jacket or something to wrap your arm for added protection then you should do it as this will give you an added chance of coming out of the altercation alive.

There are a number of ways that you can look at for blocking a knife attack. A primary issue that you need to be aware of, is that when blocking a knife it is not done in the traditional sense that you may be thinking about. Typically you cannot use a hard low, middle or high block where the arm forcefully snaps outward (usually with the arm at a 90 deg angle) to stop the incoming knife strike.

To be fair, yes it is possible to strike hard enough with the block to knock the weapon from the attackers' hand, but this is an iffy prospect and will not work every time. How often is this type of technique successful? Forty percent of the time? Fifty percent? Are you willing to gamble your life on it working for you?

This is because the knife is a 'live' weapon and not static like practiced in many traditional arts. The blade is constantly in motion or moving at a rapid pace and quickly able to change direction. If you execute a static type of block the blade wielder can easily slash your arm, change direction and seek a new target on your body before you have time to react.

'Hard style' or static blocking

This type of block is easy to go around.

If your block is not strong enough, the attack will just blast right through.

This is why speed and distance are so important and also why you need to focus on taking the fight to the attacker. The attacker needs to be stopped at all costs in order for the assault to end and for you to survive.

Having fast hands and reflexes are an essential component which will allow you to take full advantage of any window of opportunity during an attack. When you see an opening to strike you cannot hesitate and must move in quickly and decisively.

Speed drills will enhance your skills and working with a training blade will increase the velocity of your movements even more, especially if you practice with intent and don't just go through the motions. Just the fact that your partner is slashing at you with a training knife in his hand will vastly increase your speed.

Be aware that if you are in a situation where a knife is involved, you will get cut. This is a sober reality and there is no getting around it, the knife is too quick and deadly. It only takes a slight touch with the edge of the blade or a wrong move on your part. The best that you are hoping to do is to get out of the encounter alive. If you can find a way out of the situation before it begins then do it.

A final thought: for those of you who meet someone that guarantees you a surefire knife technique/disarm with no harm to your person...........run away as fast as you can because they are either lying or woefully unaware of reality.

Note: to make it more realistic, an aluminum training knife is very helpful, however, in the beginning I recommend a hard plastic or wood trainer.

Cross body blocking

Cross body blocking is the first type of 'blocking' that we teach and is used to better control a man with a blade by allowing you to keep the knife away from your body and vital areas.

When you block in this fashion, your body will twist at the waist and your arm blocks across your body from your right to your left with the palm up. This keeps the veins and arteries in the forearm away from the blade and allows you better control by providing constant pressure on his weapons hand thereby keeping the blade away from your body.

Anytime that you are attempting to block in this fashion your arm must be strong and firm but fluid as well. This blocking style is applied at middle range and it is important to be able to keep track and maintain control of the aggressors attacking hand.

Whenever you attempt to intercept a bladed attack remember that speed is essential both offensively and defensively. You will need to counter attack to the eyes, throat, groin or shin using your hands or feet as well as block or maneuver away from the attack. You cannot just block, as this is a passive gesture and you are staying on the defensive. You must turn the situation around and go on the offensive by punching or kicking if you hope to survive.

Cross Body Block

Player 'B' attacks with a slashing or thrusting attack on the high line. Player 'A' executes a Cross Body block with his right hand to stop the incoming attack.

As Player 'B' changes direction and tries to cut to the midsection, Player 'A' maintains contact and forces the blade down and away from his body.

Player 'B' comes back with a thrust or slash from his left side, Player 'A' again Cross Body blocks and as 'B' again tries to slash to the low line 'A' redirects the attack down and away from himself.

If you look at the previous pictures showing Cross Body Blocking you will see that initially, it looks like a traditional 'hard' block. The difference is in the execution of the 'block'.

When an attacker slashes at you with an edged weapon and meets an obstruction (your arm) he will simply go around it by cutting your forearm or slashing to your midsection.

If you don't maintain contact with the arm he will simply go around your block.

In order to remedy this problem after the initial 'block', you must maintain the pressure by pushing your forearm out and downward to keep the blade away from your body as shown on the previous page. As you press downward on the forearm to maintain control of the knife you also want to hollow out your midsection to further help keep the blade away.

Many people/students think that they are blocking and scooping the attacker's arm away from them, but no, that is not what you are doing. You are trying to keep the knife blade away from your midsection as the attacker changes directions with the knife to slash you on the low line.

You can try scooping if you are quick enough, but any knife wielder worth his salt, when meeting an obstruction will immediately change direction in order to cut you in a different area of the body.

Next, we have **'Meeting the Force'** because you are meeting his 'force' or attack with an attack of your own. While this works best if you have a weapon because you would actually be striking or slashing the attacker's hand, it can be applied even if you are unarmed.

When using an empty hand 'meeting the force' block you would use your fist, knuckles or elbow to inflict pain and hopefully cause him to drop his weapon while you finish him off. The idea behind this type of 'blocking' is to cause damage to the limb holding the weapon.

For example, when the opponent executes an angle #1 strike you will counter with an angle #1 thereby meeting his attack with an attack of your own, catching him on the inside forearm or wrist.

This usually starts with a Three Count blocking type of method such as a right hand, left hand, right hand, with the final move being a punch or eye jab. It is imperative that you do damage to the attacker as quickly as possible. You must turn thing around by becoming the aggressor, if you stay on the defensive you will lose.

Three Count Block

Three count block against a forehand slash. In training we use an open palm slap but in reality, this would be a hammer fist or strike with the knuckles.

61

3-count block against a backhand slash

The reason for the 3 movements is that the first strike stops the attack, the second strike grabs and controls the weapons arm and the third strike is an attack to the eyes, face, throat or other area to help to stop or at least slow down the attacker. The 2nd block can also act as a backup in case the first block misses its mark.

Following the Force

Following the Force can be a little problematic as you are 'blocking' in the same direction that the opponent is striking.

That is to say that if your opponent attacks with an angle #1 (his right to left downward diagonal strike), you would block by coming behind his strike and throwing an angle #2 (from your left to right downward diagonal).

This is more difficult because the attacker knows what strike he is going to attack with (1, 2, 3, etc...), but you have to see it, recognize it and then try to intercept it from behind.

These blocks are normally executed at long range and it is usually a little easier to catch anything coming from his left side (as in a backhand strike) or a straight thrusting angle five. Here are a few examples:

Angles #3 and #4

Angle #5

Angle #8

Straight Thrust (angle #5)

Before we finish this chapter we need to take a closer look at the straight thrust. Even though this is a common attack, very few books, videos or martial arts/self-defense courses spend any time learning to deal with the situation. Why? Because it is extremely difficult and if you let the assailant get too close it is next to impossible to defend against.

The straight thrust comes in at a low angle at about waist height. Well below the line of sight, making it extremely hard to see and deal with unless you are able to maintain proper distance. On many occasions the attacker will rush in and slam his left forearm into your chest while thrusting the blade into your midsection.

This is an extremely quick and vicious attack and almost impossible to defend against or counter. Below and later in the book, we will show some ways that may help you to deal with this attack.

Wrong: Downward circular block, this takes far too much time and you will never be able to intercept the attack in time.

Circular block: Many systems teach this block but it is way too slow to use against a thrusting knife attack. You have to move your arm in an entire half circle, but your attacker only has to thrust in a straight line a few inches to make contact.

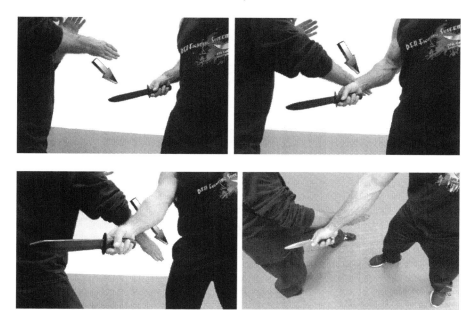

Correct: *The more efficient way would be to drive the arm in a straight line downward thereby intercepting his attack at the midpoint. It is also helpful to step offline and/or hollow out your middle.*

Shoot the hand straight downward in front of your body. This will also cause his attack to angle off as it slides along your forearm.

Downward block: *Again this block strikes straight downward not in a half circle. The idea is to smash and damage his forearm. If you get lucky it may also shock the muscles and tendons in the forearm resulting in the hand opening and causing him to lose his weapon.*

Straight Line downward block with an eye jab

Blocking to the Outside: *Remember to do this in a linear fashion and not circular.*

Blocking to the Inside

Grabbing

When being attacked in a rapid fire thrusting attack (typically called 'sewing machine attack') most people will instinctively try to grab the hand. The problem is that for most of us our reflexes are not fast enough and we are always a fraction of a second behind the attacker. When trying to grab the hand or wrist you usually end up only grabbing a fistful of air.

When being attacked in this fashion people will instinctively try to grab the hand.

A better option may be trying to grab near the elbow and not the wrist. The wrist being at the end of the arm is moving a farther distance and is a smaller target than the elbow. The attack needs to be stopped closer to the source of its origination such as the elbow or shoulder.

By trying to grab the wrist you are trying to 'time' the strike and grab a small target at the split second that it comes into view or as the blade is about to enter your abdomen. If you stretch your arms forward towards the elbow you now have the entire forearm to grab.

Shoot the hands out towards the elbow while bending at the waist (hollowing out)

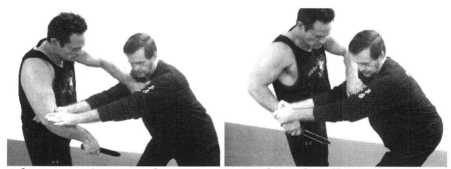

A better option may be trying to grab at the elbow and not the wrist.

Grabbing from the side

When grabbing the attackers arm from the side you must be sure to alternate your grip, which is one hand palm up and one hand palm down. If you have both hands in the same position it will be too easy for the attacker to pull free.

The weakest component of the grab is the thumb (one thumb versus four fingers) if both hands grab his arm with the thumbs down, you now have eight fingers on top of his arm and only two on the bottom. When he struggles to get his arm free it won't be too difficult to accomplish, but by simply turning one hand over you will have five fingers on the top and five fingers on the bottom. A much better advantage for you.

This grip is easy to break free from.

This is a much better choice and gives you a fighting chance.

Now even if you manage to grab the arm with one hand up and one hand down you still need to be aware of not getting too close. As stated many times throughout this book you need to cause damage to him, disarm him or control him. If you haven't done that yet you may have a problem.

If you stay too close to the assailant and haven't been able to cause injury to him yet, it will be a very simple matter for him to simply move the weapon to his other hand and continue with the attack. Another problem is that if you are on the inside (between his arms) he can easily grab and choke you.

Once you gain control of the weapon you need to stay on the outside and keep him stretched out so he cannot change hands or grab you.

From the angle #5 attack, you step offline, block and grab the arm, but be aware that

By letting the attacker keep his arms in close to his body it is an easy matter for him to change the weapon to his other hand.

It doesn't matter which side you are on you must keep his hands apart, disable or incapacitate him.

Getting in between his arms is not a good place to be unless you can quickly disable him.

Keep him stretched out

Keeping his arms stretched out so that he cannot change hands with the weapon or grab you.

Jamming

Jamming is another good option, in this way you interrupt his attack and keep him from thrusting the blade forward. Of course, a follow up is quickly needed because just jamming his arm will not be effective for very long.

This technique doesn't look like it will work, but it is actually very effective and it has the advantage of stopping the attack before it begins.

Jamming the arm

Chapter 8 - Training Drills

When performing your training drills, speed, repetition and accuracy are very important. When going up against an edged weapon your speed, both offensive and defensive is the best weapon that you have. Your window of opportunity is very brief in a knife encounter and you must be able to react and respond the instant that you see your opening.

The following drills will help to increase your speed, reaction, timing and awareness if you train properly. You will be amazed at how much working against a blade will enhance your skills, even more than practicing the drills empty hand. You need to make sure that you treat the training blade as if it were a 'live' or edged weapon. That means that you stay alert, move quickly and with proper technique.

Don't be apathetic when you go through the motions, you don't talk about work, movies or sports and you don't let the blade touch you. You may laugh but I occasionally catch students doing this very thing.

Any time that the training weapon touches any part of your body, you are cut. Have fun with it, make a game of it, but practice and practice seriously. Not just 3 or 4 times, but for 20, 30 minutes or an hour a few times a week, put the effort and time in now because on the street there is no second chance.

Be aware that no amount of skill or training will make you invincible or keep you from getting cut or stabbed. In fact, it is very likely that you will be cut so you have to move quickly, maintain the proper distance and end the situation expeditiously so that you can seek help. Keep this sobering thought in mind if you should ever find yourself in this type of circumstance and try to avoid it at all costs.

Here we will show a few training drills that you can practice to help improve your skill against the knife. When you are practicing your techniques make sure to train with intent, don't just walk through the motions.

It is best to purchase a strong, stiff training blade. It doesn't have to be an aluminum knife, a hard plastic or wooden knife is fine, but the flimsy rubber knives that many places sell will not work and will give you a false sense of confidence.

Remember: the way that you train is the way that you will react on the street.

Be sure to check out the free videos at our site to see exactly how the drills are performed.
http://bit.ly/2mFZPJJ

Evading

Before doing any blocks or counter drills you need to practice simply evading the knife attack. By using the footwork drills shown in Chapter 5, you can gain an understanding of body mechanics and how you need to move to avoid being cut.

Start off slow and start by stepping only, no hands or blocks. This will force you to concentrate on your footwork and movements in addition to training you to step far enough away to avoid the blade. When people start blocking they tend to believe that the block will be enough to deal with the attack...............it is not.

Angle #1 - When encountering an angle #1 attack, stepping back with the left foot feels wrong, but you need to get to the outside of the attacker. If you were to step with the right foot you would be moving directly into the path of the attack.

Angle #1 from a different view point

Angle #2 - *Again you are stepping to the outside*

Angle #2 *from a different view point*

Angle #3 - *Be careful of your hand placement, either have them down or up and out to the side. If your hands are up in front of your face they will likely be cut.*

Note: Putting the hands up to ward off the attack is very common (and very wrong) and the cause of what you always hear of as 'defensive wounds' at crime scenes.

Angle #4

Angle #5 *- This attack is one of the most common and most difficult to get away from.*

Angle #5

Angle #6

Angle #7

Angle #8

Angle #8 different view point

This stepping and evasion will take some time to get used to, but it is imperative that you practice your footwork drills if you want to be successful in your training and defensive measures.

We start with stepping back and avoiding the attack before we even think about using the forward angles as those take a little more skill to maneuver around the blade.

Arm Wrenching

Arm Wrenching is done to damage the arm holding the weapon. If you do not execute damage to your attacker in some fashion you will not be able to disarm him. Period!

This is the biggest mistake that people make when trying weapons counters and especially disarms. Most of you have had the experience of trying a disarming or joint locking technique on your partner when he suddenly clamps down with all of his strength thereby making it all but impossible for your counter to work.

At this point many people, especially those working on their own without the benefit of a trained instructor will decide that "This technique doesn't work" and choose to abandon it.

This line of thought is not always correct. First of all your partner should be helping you not 'fighting' you while you are trying to learn new tactics. Remember, you must crawl before you walk, walk before you run.

Secondly if you were to give your training partner a quick finger jab to the throat or eyes or a swift kick to the groin, then he will definitely loosen his grip on the weapon and making the disarm possible. People tend to forget these things.

When learning a new technique you need to slowly go over the basics and fundamentals of the counter move. Analyze it, try different scenarios or slightly different variations. Not everyone reacts or moves in the same way.

Once you feel comfortable with the drill and are confident in your ability to properly execute it successfully you can now try 'pressure testing' by adding resistance.

Hint: this procedure takes longer than 5 minutes.

Wrench #1

Using the 3-count blocking that we learned in Chapter 7, you use the right hand then left hand to stop the attack. On the 3rd beat or strike, you will be attacking the elbow joint. This is a push/pull type of motion, you push on the wrist while pulling or snapping the elbow.

Wrench #2

Off of an angle #2 strike, you would block and then use an elbow strike to his elbow while pulling on the wrist.

Wrench #3

Angle #2 or #4 attack, you would block and by swinging your arm upward you snap or hyperextend his elbow.

Wrench #4

Angle #2 or #4 attack, you can block and snap the elbow against your chest. Be sure to punch or palm the face as your arm comes across.

Wrench #5

For angles #2, #4, #6 or #8, you can also break the arm across your shoulder. You can also strike his elbow with the forearm or bicep before breaking it on the shoulder.

Notice the groin strike and be sure not to stay in this position or you will be grabbed from behind.

Note: For angles #1 & #3 using the shoulder break would put you between his arms and you can be easily grabbed therefore it is not recommended.

Disarms

Many people will tell you that a disarm cannot be done, but of course this depends on many variables, the situation, the environment, the person who is attacking and the skill of the person being attacked.

One important thing to keep in mind is that disarms are accidental or secondary techniques. You should never go into a street encounter with the intent of doing a disarm; it will just happen to be there during the course of your counter defense.

You may be wondering how you will know or see a disarm opportunity during a combative encounter, well that only comes from practice and I mean lots of practice. If you only train a drill for five minutes and then move on to the next one, you only 'think' that you know the technique, but in reality, you do not and under duress you will never be able to pull it off. The drill needs to be practiced over and over again until it is implanted into the muscle memory.

What does all of this mean? It means that if someone attacks you with a knife or any weapon and you are trying to grab his wrist to disarm the weapon then you will be cut. Your focus needs to be on stopping the attack first and then getting rid of the weapon.

If your core focal point is based on taking away the weapon then you will be too intent on grabbing it or the arm. This won't be possible because his hand and arm will be moving too fast for you to catch. You need to slow him down and disable him while trying to block the attack. If all of that works out then you may be able to disarm him.

Does that mean that you shouldn't practice disarms? No, of course not. You never know what type of situation you will find yourself in and it is always good to prepare for any scenario.

One last thing, when attempting a disarm DO NOT grab the blade. I see instructors and so-called experts teach this all of the time. They will tell you that once you grab the blade you can pull the knife away from the attacker or "It's better to have your hand cut than your throat."

Now, this line of thinking is obviously flawed. One problem is that very few people can consciously hold onto a blade while it is slicing into their flesh. It is a razor sharp piece of metal that you are grabbing, once it starts to dig into your skin and muscle tissue your hand will automatically open.

I see students grab the blade all of the time while trying to disarm and it drives me nuts. I can't imagine why they think that this is a good idea. Additionally, it is no problem for the attacker to grab your wrist with one hand and pull the blade through your fingers with the other hand. Even with a training weapon you can accomplish this quite easily.

DO NOT GRAB THE BLADE!

It is a simple matter for the attacker to push your arm away while pulling the blade through your hand.

Now that I've gotten that out of my system here are some basic disarms for you to try.

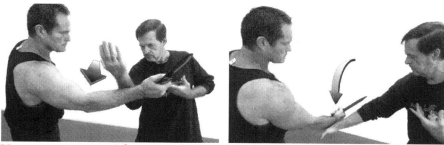

You can start with a pendulum block or any way that you would like to start.

Here I'm blocking, cutting to the neck and then starting the disarm

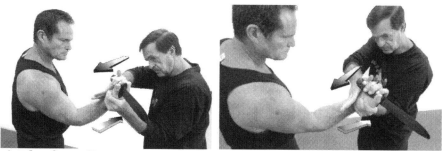

1) The first disarm uses the butt end of the handle. This is an option that people rarely think about and can only be done with large knives (otherwise the handle is too short and will not protrude from the bottom of the hand).

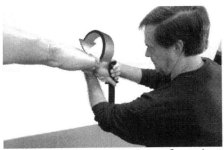

2) *Here is a variation showing the same disarm from the other side. Notice how I am twisting his arm in the opposite direction.*

3) *You can also push on the blade to dislodge the handle from his hand.*

4 & 5) *Here are two variations of the strip, one using the back of the forearm and the other grabbing as low to the handle as possible. You need a firm grip on the meaty part of the thumb to make these disarms work.*

Push straight down using the back of the hand or forearm, if done properly the knife falls into your hand.

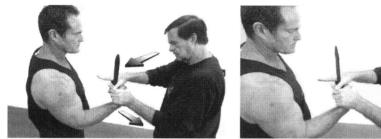

6) Here you use the web of the hand and push forward while pulling with the left hand. If you look closely you will see that I am applying a wrist flex while disarming.

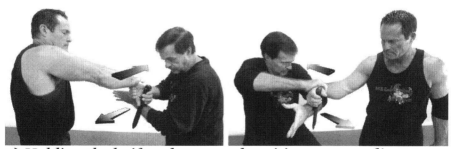

7) Holding the knife a downward position you can disarm with the forearm

8) *Or instead of pushing the blade straight out where the knife would be free for anyone to pick up you can bring it into your chest for better control.*

9) *With the knife still in the downward position, you disarm with your palm up. Again this allows the handle to drop right into your palm as you push the knife forward.*

10) *Return to Sender: in this variation, you actually shove the blade into the attackers' rib cage and pull his hand free while the knife is lodged in his ribs.*

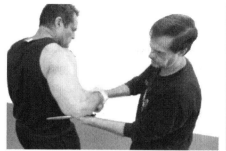

In practice you place the blade of the knife at the small of the back and quickly pull his hand, ripping the knife free.

11) *For this last one you need to execute the Pendulum block and scoop the arm clockwise*

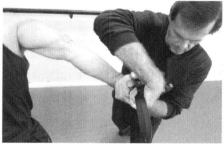

Bringing the arm all the way around so that he ends up in a reverse wrist flex

Reach over and rip the knife from his grasp, be sure to keep twisting and keeping pressure on the thumb or 'gatekeeper' as it is typically called in Southeast Asian arts.

Note: All of these disarms require a Push/Pull action in order for them to work. You need to Push the knife while Pulling on the hand.

Percussion Strike Disarms

Percussion strikes are a little tricky to pull off, but can be very effective if you get good at it. As you grip the attacker's hand or wrist you will apply a forceful slap to the back of his hand. If done properly the force of the blow will 'pop' his hand open and release the knife.

I was training in the Philippines when I first learned this type of disarm and I had a terrible time getting the technique down. I would slap my partner's hand 6-8 times until I could get it to open up. It went on like this for a few days (much to my partners displeasure) until during one training session I suddenly blocked his attack, grabbed his wrist and BLAM, the technique felt nice, clean and crisp and the knife flew from his hand and stuck into the ground (we were training outdoors).

It was just a matter of constant practice until it suddenly 'clicked'. After that, it was easy to accomplish the disarm every time.

1) Percussion strike in the high position using the open palm

2) Using the elbow to strike the hand (this one works really well)

3) *Using the palm in the downward position*

4) *Double strike used against an angle #5, hitting the wrist and back of the hand.*

Angle Eight Drill (vertical downward strike)

This drill is done with the knife in the reverse or ice pick position. As your partner delivers the downward strike you immediately angle to your right while throwing up your left arm to block. You never want to stay directly under an incoming knife attack, always angle away from the attack or shift offline.

Your arm comes up at a 45 degree angle not perpendicular and you immediately grab his wrist and twist the arm downward. The flat of the blade is positioned on the outside of the forearm. When his arm reaches the point when it will not twist any farther you continue your motion by slightly loosening your grip. This allows your hand to keep sliding and your forearm will push the blade out of his hand.

This is the basic move only and it is always preceded by a strike of some sort. When we train we will use a firm strike the chest with a palm strike to simulate a finger jab to the eyes or throat. The palm strike should be strong enough to jolt your partner.

Variation 1

Player 'A' on the left attacks player 'B' with a downward vertical strike, the knife is in the Reverse grip. Player 'B' angles offline to his right while simultaneously blocking upward.

Note: When training this drill it is a good idea to palm strike (with enough contact to jolt him) your partner in the chest to simulate a strike to the eyes or throat at the same time as you block. Stepping offline, blocking and the right hand strike to the chest should be executed at the same time.

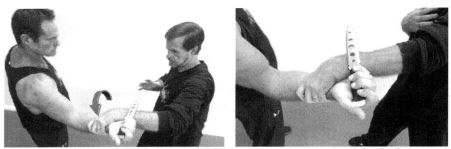

Player 'B' continues to twist the wrist (notice the blade laying on the back of the forearm)

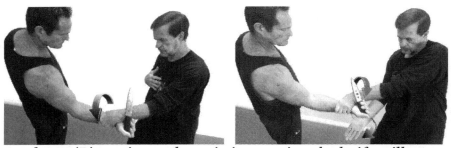

As player 'B' continues the twisting motion the knife will start to peel away from player 'A's hand.

Notice how player 'B' has his right hand underneath to catch the knife as it falls free. You will probably catch it in a Forward or Hammer grip position, but simply switch it to a Reverse grip and launch the same attack back to your partner. This allows both players to get a workout.

Variation 2

Part 2 starts off exactly the same as the previous drill. Player 'A' on the left attacks player 'B' with a downward vertical strike. Player 'B' angles offline to his right while simultaneously blocking upward.

Player 'B' continues to twist the wrist (notice the blade laying on the back of the forearm)

As player 'B' continues the twisting motion the knife will start to peel away from player 'A's hand.

Here is where things change. Instead of disarming the knife into your right hand as before, you will use your right hand to grab the meaty part of the thumb, squeeze as hard as you can and continue the twisting motion. This will help to loosen his grip and allow you to strip the knife free with your **left** hand.

Continue twisting as you pull straight back with your left hand

Try to grab as close to the handle as you can. Do not grab the blade.

If you do it properly the knife should pull free with the handle/grip falling right into your hand. Switch the knife to your right hand and continue the drill.

Note: This variation is used when the attacker is too strong and variation #1 will not work.

Variation 3

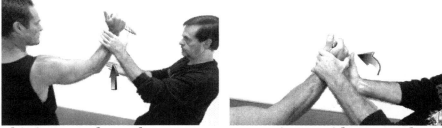

This is a tough one because you are trying to sidestep and catch the attacking hand at the same time, but it can be done. As you move offline to avoid the blade you need to let the knife arm come to you.

Don't chase it or try to grab it. If you look closely you will see that my right hand is at waist or chest height and my left hand is guiding it into my right hand.

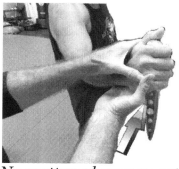 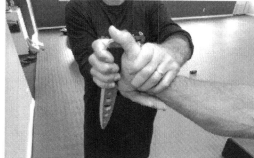

No matter where you catch the arm you need to slide your hands down to the wrist for better control.

 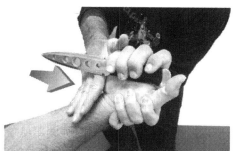

Using your left hand you will execute a wrist flex will help to loosen his grip while you slide the right hand up and over his fingers to remove the knife. Be sure to keep your hand flat as I am doing here.

 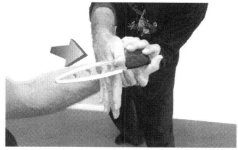

By pushing your hand forward this will cause the handle to end up in your hand. All of these disarms use a push/pull motion. While you are pushing the knife out of his hand your other hand is pulling. DO NOT grab the blade.

Hint: If you are having trouble catching the knife in the proper position it is probably because your partner is not aiming at your chest. Many students will unintentionally aim off to the side so as not to hurt their training partner. Don't Do This!

To make the drill realistic you Must aim for the chest.

Pad Drills

Pad drills allow you to add a bit of realism to your training by giving you the opportunity to go all out with your technique. You can punch, elbow or knee the pad as hard as you can without fear of injuring your training partner.

Drill 1

1) Parry the angle #5 while stepping offline and quickly grabbing with your right hand

Keeping control of the arm, step in and punch multiple times to the face (pad).

Drill 2

2) Again with the straight thrust you slam your downward block into his forearm (you could also parry with your right hand instead) and grab his wrist.

Move his weapon out away from your body and throw multiple shots to the midsection.

These are just two examples and you should feel free to create many more. Just be sure to keep them realistic.

Passing Drill

Pass & Scoop Drill - The idea of this drill is to teach you how to move your opponents' limbs out of your way so that you can close the gap and enter into close range while still controlling his weapons hand in order to allow you to finish your counterattack.

1) You want to stop the initial attack with your outside angled block (left hand) or 3-count blocking (right, left, right). Then you will immediately bring the right hand under and Pass it overhead in order to move to the outside and away from the knife. This can be done the opposite way also off of an angle #2

2) Another way to Pass his arm is to use the same hand. After momentarily stopping his attack

You fold your arm under his arm and Pass it overhead, regain control and disable.

3) Scooping is what you will need for the Pendulum Drill shown a little later and is the same as the Cross Body Blocking that we did in Chapter 7.

Remember to keep the pressure on so that the blade cannot touch you.

4) *Once you feel comfortable with blocking and passing you can start adding disarms*

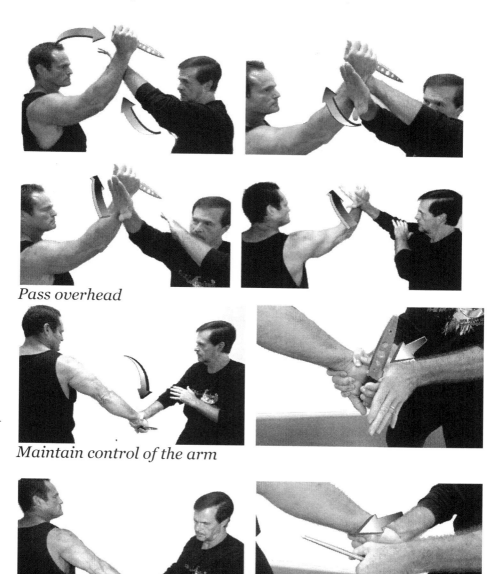

Pass overhead

Maintain control of the arm

Twist the wrist and push forward to disarm

 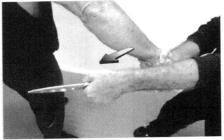

Blocking and Passing with the Knife in the Reverse Grip

5) Blocking and passing in the reverse grip position

Block and pass

Maintain a tight grip on his hand and disarm

Scooping Drill

Here's a nice drill that allows you to work angle#2 and get in a lot of repetition.

Player 'B' attacks with an angle #2. Player 'A' momentarily stops it with his left hand and using his right hand comes up underneath the attacker's arm

Passing it overhead and in a complete counter-clockwise circle (this helps you to train controlling the arm), when you complete the circle you will reach out and grab the fleshy part of his thumb (gatekeeper) with your left hand

From here you apply a wrist flex to loosen his grip

And pushing forward you will disarm the knife, slice his forearm on the way back (to always remind yourself to inflict damage on your attacker), flip the knife to a reverse grip and return a number 2 strike. This will now allow your partner to do the drill and this way both of you are getting to practice.

Pendulum Drill: Cross Body Blocking

The Pendulum drill is a good drill for helping to increase your speed, timing and reflexive action against an attack. It may go by different names, but most Southeast Asian arts have this drill or something very similar.

When I teach this at seminars (if they are not familiar with it) I have them pair up, one with a training knife and one without. Then I tell the attacker to try to slash his partner as many times as he can in 1 minute and to keep count. After one minute everyone is surprised at how many times they were cut.

Then we teach the basics of the Pendulum Drill and try the exercise again. Even though they still get cut it is always substantially lower for everyone. They are usually cut half the amount as before or less.

The drill can become very involved and very painful because you are constantly crashing your forearms together. If you are new to it then I would recommend that you use forearm pads if you have any.

The goal of your training partner is to be your teacher. His goal is not to see how many times that he can cut you, that only helps to feed his ego, doesn't help you, and only leads to a frustrating training session.

The person attacking starts with an attack to the neck or chest then switches to the stomach and finally comes back in from the other side. It actually will look like he is making a giant U-shape with the knife.

If you remember in the blocking section we talked about maintaining control and keeping the pressure constant.

Part 1 - Begin the Drill

Part 1- *To start the drill your partner (with the knife in the forward position) comes in with an angle #1 or a high thrust (similar to a hook). You begin with your cross body block*

And as your partner tries to change direction and slice your stomach (think of a U-shape)

You will maintain the forward pressure while at the same time hollowing out your midsection as an added precaution.

Your partner then comes back with an angle #2 or a high backhand thrust which you again block and scoop to the outside.

Not like this: (make sure to maintain control on the backside) Be sure to keep the hand that is not being used at your chest level so that it is in the position to block if needed and it keeps it out of the path of the blade.

This part of the drill is repeated over and over, you don't just practice it a few times and then move on to something else. It needs to become a reflexive motion and worked into the muscle memory, a good way to make sure that you get enough repetition is to set a timer for 5-10 minutes to start and work up to 15-20 minutes or keep working until your forearms can no longer take the pain.

One thing that I want to stress is that you are not using brute force in this drill, you are looking for speed so your shoulders need to relax. There should be no tension. You want to move and block as fast as you can.

Yes, there will be some force and arm pain as you are constantly 'banging' your forearms together but using force is not the goal. You are looking to enhance your speed and reflex action. This is a tough concept for most people to grasp if you do not have an experienced teacher around to help you.

Part 2 - Take the hand away

Part 2 - *As the drill continues, occasionally (not every time) the trainer will reach across and slap the blocking hand away*

When this happens you will immediately replace it with your left hand to avoid getting your belly sliced open and retain control of the weapon

In order to maintain the cross body blocking structure, you quickly shoot the right hand back in place and continue the drill. The left hand is only there for a moment to keep his arm in place until you can get the right hand back into position. It is difficult to block an attack coming from your left side with only your left hand as it is very easy for the attacker to slide down your forearm and cut your midsection.

Notice how the training partner is reaching UNDER his arm in order to remove the block. If he were to reach over his arm he may cut his own wrist.

Occasionally (again, don't do it every time or you develop a rhythm) the attacking partner will do the same thing on the left side that is pull your blocking arm away causing you to repeat the same quick 1,2 blocking that you did earlier.

The reason that the defender needs to get the left hand back into place is to maintain the cross body blocking structure.

#3 - Adding a punch

For the third and final section (for now) the attacker will occasionally throw a left hook punch at your head. You must try to block this punch in addition to monitoring the knife that is still swinging in your direction.

This can get a bit complicated, but is also a lot of fun to drill.

Part 3 - Adding a punch

Blocking the left hook and quickly swinging the arm over to execute a cross body block

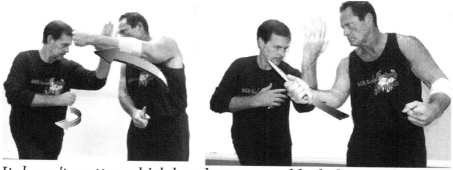

It doesn't matter which hand you use to block the punch just try not to get hit or cut.

Notes

Knife Flow Drill

This is a nice little flow drill that has about ten moves in it (depending on how you count) that helps you to practice your stepping, parrying, blocking, joint locking and disarms.

It's actually pretty easy to learn and students can usually pick up the whole thing in one class session. If you are having trouble with this or any of the drills, click on or go to the link below to view the videos and see how they are executed.

http://bit.ly/2mFZPJJ

Player 'B' begins with an angle #5 thrusting attack. Player 'A' steps offline and parries the arm

Shoot in the sliding downward block to help move the knife away from you while you grab his arm at the elbow with your left hand.

While maintaining control of the arm Player 'A' drives an elbow strike into the forearm

From here Player 'A' grabs the hand and executes 'Return to Sender'

Next, you pull the arm out and break it across your chest as you forearm strike to the throat (for safety you will hit your partner in the chest on this move).

Since you have never let go of the wrist with your right hand, fold his arm into a Figure 4 lock as you sharply snap your forearm or ridge hand into the crease of his elbow. This strike will help to bend the arm.

After the figure 4 you can slice the side of his neck by pulling his arm forward.

Move back to the figure 4 position and transition it into a Reverse Figure 4 (keep your head tucked so you do not get punched).

Holding his hand and applying pressure with your left hand you can disarm the knife from here and you slip your left arm into a Cradle lock.

Finish with a stab to the heart and then reverse the knife in your hand and attack with a number 5 thrust. This will reverse the roles and now allow your partner to run through the flow drill.

Note: This is what is called a Flow Drill. It is NOT a fighting technique or counter. It is actually many counters put together to teach you how to flow from technique to technique.

Chapter 9 - Street Defense Techniques

The best defense is situational awareness, to be aware of your surroundings, especially at night or in a questionable area of town. It is always best to avoid violence, but that is not always possible, sometimes despite your best efforts, it finds you.

This doesn't mean that you have to be paranoid, just use common sense. Don't walk alone at night in dark unlit areas, if you are in a restaurant or building, note where the exits are in case of an emergency, keep your car doors locked while driving, these are things that we've all heard it before, but many people don't pay heed to these safe practices or they think that it will never happen to them. The news is full of stories containing people who say "I never thought this would happen to me."

We are our own biggest obstacle when it comes to street defense and our own safety. We never dream that anything bad will happen to us or that we will become the victim of a crime. Most people are decent, hard-working members of the community who only want to get an education, find a nice job, get married, raise a family, enjoy life and then retire.

Unfortunately, not everyone thinks this way, not everyone shares the same ideas and values that most normal people have. There are those who only want to take from you and from society as a whole, they feel entitled or owed something, are on drugs or simply don't care.

They have no morals, no values, no compassion, and no empathy towards their fellow man. They live on the fringe of society and they see you as prey, simply another victim to use, take from and discard. This may seem harsh and some of you don't want to believe it, but it is a reality.

Many self-defense books, articles and experts will tell you to reason with them, perhaps this will work, but many of them are not reasonable people, they don't want to talk, they don't want a lecture, they want your money or your body to rape and or murder.

These people don't play or live by the same rules as the rest of us, so what would seem like a normal response to an assault may not work. If you can just hand over your wallet, phone or purse, then by all means do it, you can always make more money and credit cards can be replaced, but unfortunately, sometimes that isn't enough.

If it seems that you or your loved one's life is in danger then you cannot be indecisive, you must attack. If you delay, hesitate, or stop to think about doing something, you will start to lose your nerve.

The counter attack must be swift and violent, and you must attack with twice as much aggression as the attacker has shown. In an evenly matched encounter, the person who is more aggressive will usually be victorious.

Knife defense skills are essential in today's society, considering that many people carry weapons on their person, but it is not only knives that can be a problem. A knife, axe, scissors, screwdriver or box cutter can all be used for stabbing or slashing.

Unarmed defense against a knife or ANY weapon is extremely difficult and actually not advised unless you have no other alternative. No matter how much training you have or how good you think that you are, it is always best to avoid any altercation dealing with a blade.

If you try to disarm a knife, gun, a length of pipe, hammer or any weapon there is a good chance that you will be seriously injured or killed; avoidance is always the best policy.

In a knife fight, there are no winners, everyone gets cut or stabbed. What we are discussing is trying to alleviate the immediate threat so that we can make our escape.

Being confronted with a knife is always scary and always dangerous, but if it does happen there are a few things to remember:

Stay calm by breathing deeply, you can also try clenching and unclenching your hands so that you don't 'freeze' up. Some fear is normal and helps you to stay alert, heightens the senses and keeps you from doing something foolish, but too much can be an obstruction and may have a tendency to immobilize you.

Watch the assailant's shoulders or chest, by looking in this area you can use your peripheral vision to monitor the arms and hands. When the attack starts, the shoulders will move first.

You don't want to stare them in the eyes because they may be an extremely cold, cruel and intimidating looking person, and this could incapacitate your ability to react.

Additionally, if you are staring at their eyes and then quickly start looking around for a way out, your eyes will give away your intention to attempt something.

Same thing with the weapon, the more that you stare at it the more frightening and 'larger' it becomes.

Knife attacks are not like in the movies and not like what you practice in a self-defense class. No one will execute one thrust towards your midsection and then stop and 'pose' for you while you execute your technique.

However, with this being said, this is usually the best way to start learning your defensive techniques. You need to start out slowly and carefully. Get the movements down correctly, focus on the angle of the attack, your footwork, body shifting, blocking and counter attack.

This needs to be done hundreds of times before trying to speed it up or resist your partner. Too many people want to go from zero to sixty, that is to say immediately after learning a technique they want to try to resist, making it 'realistic'. You are not ready at this point because you have not yet put the time in on your training and someone will get hurt.

There are two different types of scenarios that may occur when encountering an assailant with a knife, a knife threat and a knife attack.

A **knife threat,** is one where the assailant has brandished the weapon and is holding it in a threatening position against your body or at your neck. The aggressor is holding the knife in close proximity to your body to use as leverage to get something from you. He may or may not attack. At this stage you can comply with his demands or execute a quick and aggressive attack of your own to disable the opponent and dislodge or control the knife.

A **knife attack** means that the hands are in motion, the attacker is moving towards you with the weapon with the intent of doing you bodily harm. He is no longer talking or making demands. At this point, you must escape if you can (you may be cornered) or fight back and defend yourself. This is where your training comes into play (yes you must train in order to be effective), you cannot just read this book or watch a video and even remotely believe that you can defend yourself in a knife encounter.

When you are training remember to try different environments such as a stairway, office, restaurant or even a car. Strike his vital targets, use body shifting to avoid the blade and don't forget your footwork. Time and again I see students just stand there when the attack comes in thinking that their blocking arm will do the job. It won't. You need to move your feet and your body to maintain a safe range and avoid getting stabbed. Remember it only takes a touch with an edged weapon.

If you are accosted on the street, then it is up to you to fight back and protect yourself. You can't depend on passersby (how many stories have you read about someone being attacked and onlookers standing around doing nothing to help them) and you can't depend on the police, they can't be everywhere and by the time that they get to you it will be too late.

You have to do everything in your power to get away from an assailant; if you are dragged into a car or van the chances of getting out alive are not good.

Remember; No one has the right to touch, molest or assault you.

Here we'll show a variety of techniques for you to experiment with. For now, do the technique or drill as shown, but later the drills will change according to how your opponent reacts. That is the hardest thing for people to understand, they want you to give them a set of techniques or counter attacks to use not realizing that it doesn't work that way.

You can only react to what you are given, you may have the intention of putting him in an arm bar, but if he resists too violently and tries to stand up you will need to employ something else like a figure 4. You cannot dictate your opponent's reactions to your hits and strikes, you can only respond.

Even though your attackers' reactions will vary and everyone reacts differently to stimuli you have to start somewhere and the scenarios' that follow are a good place to start.

Click on or go to the link below to view the videos of the Drills and Techniques shown in this book and see how they are done.
http://bit.ly/2mFZPJJ

Hold up Scenarios

Scenario 1

Scenario 1) Player 'A' grabs Player 'B's shoulder and places a knife in his midsection in an attempt to rob him.

Player 'B' hollows out his midsection while simultaneously bringing his hands straight up and catching his weapons hand in the web of both hands and shifting to his right.

From here 'B' will quickly apply a wrist flex. Most people teach it the way shown here using both thumbs, but that is not the best way to apply this technique.........

If you try using your left thumb and place the palm of your right hand on the back of his hand and fingers while pushing at a 45 degree angle I think that you will find that you are able to apply much more pressure and pain to your partner.

Continue the wrist flex and take 'A' to the ground. Remember to bend your knees and drop your weight and center of gravity. Don't just bend at the waist.

Scenario 2

Scenario 2) Player 'A' grabs Player 'B's shoulder and this time puts the knife to his throat.

      Your hands should already be up in position as if to say "Take it easy, I don't want any trouble". Move your shoulders and neck back as far as you can (even half an inch is enough) to get the point of the blade away from your throat while grabbing his hand.

Immediately push the knife to your right in order to slash his arm that is holding your shoulder.

Now snap it to your left and apply another wrist flex.

Scenario 3

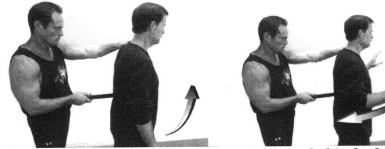

Scenario 3) Player 'A' grabs Player 'B' from behind while placing the knife in the middle of his back.

Quickly spin to your right to knock the knife away

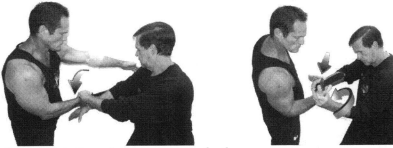

And grab his hand the same as before

If possible you can again cut his arm that is holding onto you before applying the wrist flex.

Scenario 4

Scenario 4) This time the attacker is behind you BUT the knife is being jabbed into your ribs from the side.

Quickly thrust your right forearm back and jam the knife into his midsection

While using the forearm to keep the knife in place you quickly grab his hand and pull it free

Now you can either grab the knife with either hand or continue with a wrist flex to take him to the ground.

Scenario 5

Scenario 5) Same scenario as #4 except that this time the blade of the knife is in front of your arm

Twisting to the left, you use your left hand to grab and push his hand into his midsection. Your right arm will slide past the blade as you twist and yes, you may get cut.

Press the knife to his body with your free hand and pull the hand holding the weapon away.

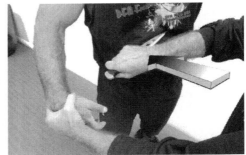

Grab the knife and cut to the midsection.

Scenario 6

Scenario 6) Again from behind with the knife to the side of your throat (note that there is a large gap between your bodies)

Quickly turn to the right bringing your right arm up and behind. You should also step out with your left foot to move yourself away from the knife.

Scoop the arm down in a clockwise manner and grabbing the thumb (gatekeeper) use the underhand disarm practiced earlier.

Angle #8 - Vertical Attacks

Vertical Attack #1

Attack 1) *Player 'B' attacks with an angle #8 in the reverse grip. Player 'A' blocks and shifts to his right while striking to the throat (change this to a palm strike to the chest for practice).*

From here Player 'A' grabs with his left hand and sharply brings his right hand down striking the crease of the elbow to cause the arm to bend.

Stepping with the left foot Player 'A' moves behind the attacker and is able to strip the knife, finish by stabbing to the kidneys.

Vertical Attack #2

Attack 2) *Starting off the same as before, you block, shift your body and strike to the throat. Grab and strike the elbow just as you did in the prior scenario.*

This time slide in so that his arm is resting on your shoulder while maintaining the backward pressure on the arm/shoulder. Punch to the face

And slide your arm through and along the side of his neck. Push against the neck while pulling on the arm as hard as you can (but not when practicing). Be sure to keep the arm bent so that you tear the rotator cuff.

Vertical Attack #3

Attack 3) This one will start off just like the angle #8 drill, variation #2 in Chapter 8

As the attacker strikes in a downward attack, you step offline, block, grab and twist. From here you reach under to grab the thumb to allow you to keep twisting and increase the pain just a bit more.

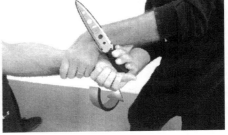

Slide the left hand back

In order to disarm the knife

Maintain the grip with your right hand after the disarm and

Insert your arm forming a cradle lock (notice how your right hand is tucking his arm under your armpit).

Now that you have his arm tied up you simply backhand thrust to the midsection.

Vertical Attack #4

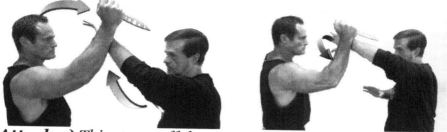

Attack 4) *This starts off the same as the previous scenario. Block, grab, twist....*

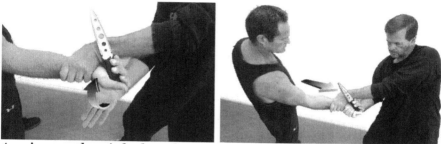

Again use the right hand to control his hand

Twist and strip the knife free

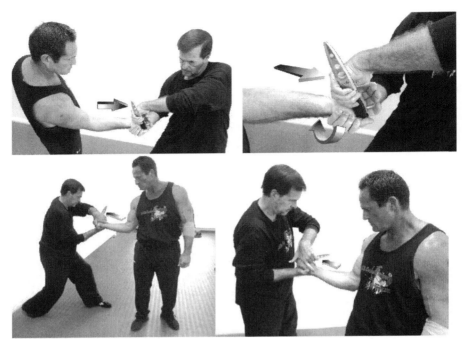

Other viewpoint

Once again you apply the Cradle to lock up his arm

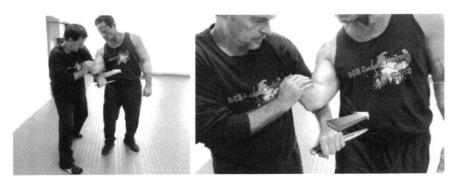

But this time as you attempt to stab him, he blocks the attack with his free hand.

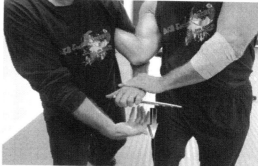

However, you have a free hand also and simply drop the knife into your right hand

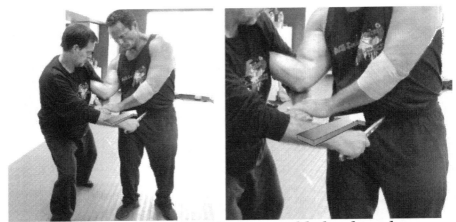

And finish your counter attack. You could also drop down and cut the leg so that he cannot grab your hand again.

Angle #1 - Diagonal Attacks (Right to Left)

Diagonal Attack (Right to Left) #1

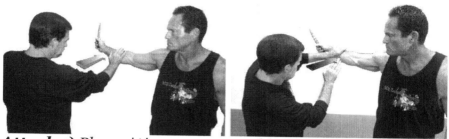

Attack 1) *Player 'A' uses a 3-count block(right, left, throat jab) to stop the attack*

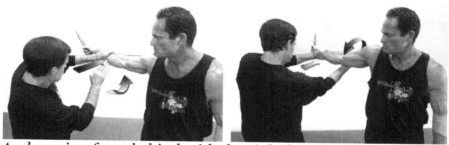

And coming from behind with the right hand 'A' sharply strikes the inside of the elbow

Causing it to bend, he quickly shoots the arm through and grabs the far side of Player 'B's neck

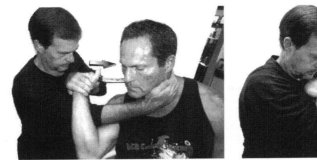

Laying the left arm against his chest Player 'A' uses his body weight to push the knife into the attackers' neck while pulling with his right hand.

Diagonal Attack *(Right to Left)* #2

Attack 2) *As Player 'A' attacks with an angle #1 or #8 Player 'B' steps offline and parries the attack while striking with a back knuckle strike to the bicep or forearm.*

Sliding the right hand down the arm 'B' grabs the wrist and throws a palm strike to the face. Next he pushes the palm under the nose and drives the attackers head back.

Driving him to the ground (at this point he could also drive the left knee into the small of the back)

149

After slamming him to the ground Player 'B' can strike to the head or neck before slamming his knee into Player 'A's neck (to hold him down) and breaking his arm across his thigh or hip.

There shouldn't be too much resistance at this point so 'B' can disarm the knife

And finish off his attacker.

Diagonal Attack (Right to Left) #3

Attack 3) Using the same technique as before Player 'B' parries, strikes the arm

Grabs the wrist and palms the face, a palm under the nose pushing him back and hyper extending the elbow, but

Instead of a takedown 'B' quickly changes to a figure 4 lock cutting him as the knife slides along the neck (changing direction in this fashion will keep the attacker off balance)

Continue with the takedown (you never want to try to hold someone in this position)

Since he is still controlling the arm he inserts the knife into the attackers' neck.

Note: be sure to step across the body with the right foot to keep the attacker from struggling and lessen the chance of him getting out of the lock.

Diagonal Attack (Right to Left) #4

Attack 4) *Player 'B' attacks with an angle #1, Player 'A' moves offline, parries and punches to the ribs (this is all 1 move, not 3 moves)*

Grabbing the weapon hand 'A' strikes with a forearm strike (similar to a clothesline strike) to the back of the head thereby jarring the brain stem.

'A' then reaches around grabbing the chin and snaps the head back

Slamming him to the ground, here he breaks the arm across his thigh and finishes with more punches if needed.

Diagonal Attack *(Right to Left)* #5

Attack 5) *Player 'A' attacks with an angle #1 while Player 'B' parries and back knuckle strikes to the forearm*

Grabbing the arm he then pulls the arm towards him while striking the bicep with an elbow strike to deaden the muscle.

'Elbow strike from both views'

Stepping out with his left foot 'B' then disarms with his left hand

Using an arm drag at the elbow 'B' takes the attacker to the ground

And finishes with an elbow strike

Diagonal Attack *(Right to Left) #6*

Attack 6) *As before we have an angle #1 attack that is parried*

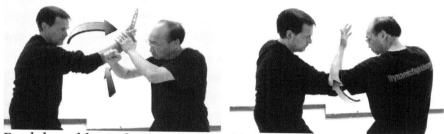

Back knuckle to the forearm and left elbow to the bicep

Again 'B' disarms with the left hand but this time

He drops down and performs a single leg takedown by placing his elbow in the hip flexor

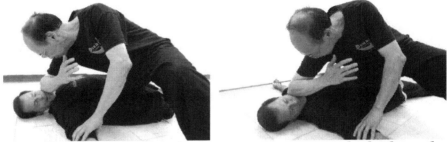

Immediately after the takedown, maneuver up the body and elbow to the face.

Diagonal Attack *(Right to Left) #7*

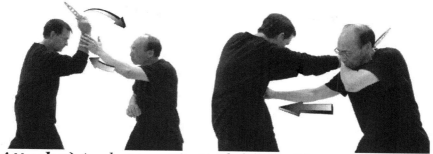

Attack 7) Angle #1 or #8 attack followed by

A disarm with the right hand

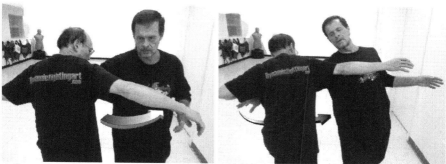

After the disarm Player 'B' steps forward and clotheslines the attacker to the throat (hit the chest in your training)

Scooping the arm and changing hands 'B' steps behind to choke the attacker from the rear

Notice how 'B' is grabbing the bottom of 'A's shirt to help pull him to the ground

Here he applies a rear choke and then leaves the scene.

Diagonal Attack *(Right to Left)* #8

Attack 8) *From the angle #1 attack player 'A' parries and blocks*

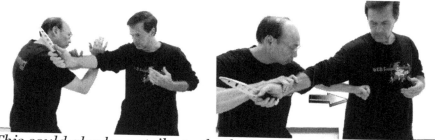

This could also be a strike to the forearm, triceps or ribs, and then he grabs the wrist and punches to the ribs

Pulling sharply at the crook of the elbow while also pushing the hand he folds the attackers arm and cuts the side of the neck

If it is a double edged blade you can slice both sides.

Diagonal Attack *(Right to Left)* #9

Attack 9) Again from the angle #1 attack 'A' parries,

Blocks and punches to the ribs

After grabbing the wrist and shoulder he then kicks to the side of the knee (hopefully breaking it) and then applies an arm bar

Taking him to the ground

'A' shifts his body weight to his opponent to keep him in place (this is important) while applying pressure to the elbow to hyper extend the joint

After damaging the arm he disarms the knife and finishes with a strike to the neck.

NOTE: If Player 'A' were to simply sit next to Player 'B' without shifting his weight onto the attacker and without applying pressure to the elbow

It would be a simple matter for 'B' to twist his body and pull his arm free, enabling him to continue his attack.

Diagonal Attack *(Right to Left) #10*

Attack 10) *From the angle #1 strike Player 'A' uses a cross body block and scoops the arm down and away*

Grabbing above the elbow with the left hand he executes and elbow strike to the bicep

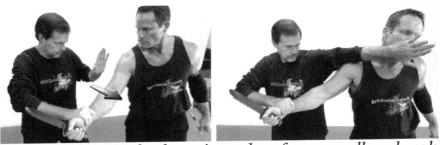

Player 'A' then, grabs the wrist and performs an elbow break across his chest while executing a palm smash to the face

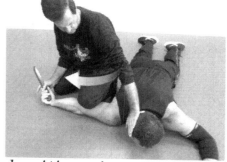

Since his arms are already in place 'A' goes into an arm bar taking the attacker to the ground. He kneels on the arm and strikes to the head

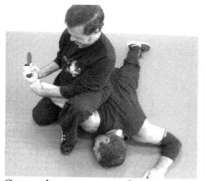

Stepping across the arm for better control 'A' pulls upward breaking the elbow and disarms the knife.

If you look closely you will notice that the first few moves (up until the takedown) are straight out of the Knife Flow Drill from Chapter 8

This is to show you how parts of the drills can be applied to real situations.

Notes

Angle #2 - Diagonal Attacks (Left to Right)

Diagonal Attack (Left to Right) #1

Attack 1) *Player 'B' swings from the left throwing an angle #2 or #4 Player 'A' executes a block and palm strike to the face*

Changing his grip to his left hand he tries for a disarm

Before the disarm can be completed Player 'B' throws a left punch, but since 'A' still has control of the knife he simply uses it to cut the arm of the incoming punch

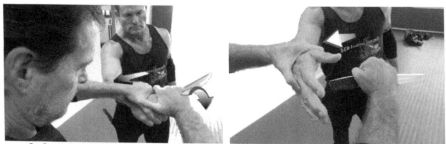

And then continues with the disarm.

Diagonal Attack *(Right to Left)* #2

Attack 2) *Player 'B' coming in with an angle #2 attack from his left, Player 'A' simultaneously blocks and throws a finger strike to the eyes. Next, he snaps the elbow against his chest*

Keeping control he then wraps his left arm around the arm that he just broke and applies more pressure. Note that 'A's left hand is grabbing his own forearm to lock the arm in tight.

From here he drops straight down to off-balance and force his opponent to the ground

Disarms and throws away the knife

And finishes with an elbow strike to the head.

Angle #5 - Straight Thrust Attacks

Straight Thrust Attack #1

Attack 1) *Player 'A' grabs Player 'B's shoulder and thrusts the knife forward towards his midsection. Player 'B' drives his arm straight down to intercept the attack and throws a finger jab to the throat (this could also go to the eyes but in this case, the attacker is wearing glasses)*

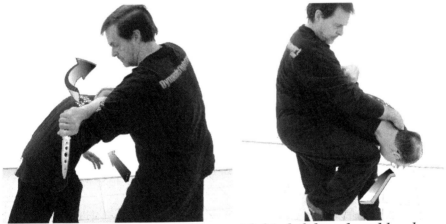

Player 'B' continues the motion with his left hand and hooks the arm holding the knife while pushing down on the back of the neck and driving a knee into his face.

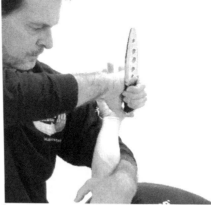

While maintaining the arm lock he disarms the knife

And finishes with a cut to the neck.

Straight Thrust Attack #2

Attack 2) *Player 'A' grabs Player 'B's shoulder and stabs straight to the midsection. Player 'B' shoots his arm forward into the armpit and locking the arm out. Also notice that his left leg is moved back to create space.*

This will not stop him for long so Player 'B' quickly jabs a finger thrust into the throat

And blocks down to angle the knife away from his body. He quickly steps to the left while grabbing the wrist with his left hand

Bringing the arm up and over into a wrist flex to cause pain and help to loosen his grip

Using the percussion disarm, sharply strike the back of the hand while continuing to hold the wrist flex

Player 'B' keeps holding the wrist lock and continues the forward motion with the right arm bringing it through into an inverted arm lock. From here 'B' can slam him backward to the ground.

Notes

Knife Stealing

If you were to ever be attacked and get caught without your weapon you can always borrow one...............from your attacker.

Knife Stealing as far as I know is unique to Southeast Asian martial arts. I am not aware of any other arts that teach these techniques which are usually taught at advanced levels if at all.

You may have seen demonstrations or videos of KunTao, Silat or FMA practitioners employing a variety of what may look like ineffective slapping motions along with their strikes.

They are not just slapping the attacker's body for the fun of it, they are looking for weapons. They will usually smack the body around the waistline and if they feel something then the shirt is quickly lifted and the object is grabbed.

This could apply to a gun or knife. Now of course if the knife is in the pocket you don't have time to try to extract it from him. This would only apply to a weapon that is easily seen and readily available.

The victim spots the attacker's knife and 'borrows' it from him.

Here we will show the knife on the outside of the shirt for clarity.

Scenario 1

Scenario 1) *When Player 'A' throws a right jab, Player 'B' parries the punch and angles offline to the attackers right.*

As Player 'B' drives an elbow into the ribs he notices the knife in the waistband. Quickly he extracts the knife

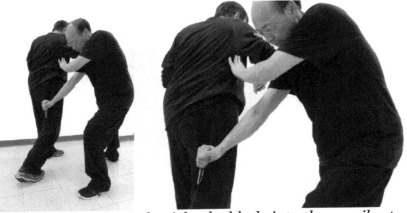

And stepping through sticks the blade into the assailants hamstring muscle

This will make it difficult for the attacker to follow and you can run to safety.

Scenario 2

Scenario 2) *When Player 'A' throws a right hook, Player 'B' blocks by driving his elbow into the biceps and*

Scooping the arm angles offline to the attackers right

Seeing the knife 'B' withdraws it from its location and strikes the kidney

Scenario 3

Scenario 3) *When Player 'A' throws a right hook, Player 'B' blocks by driving his elbow into the biceps and scoops the arm down*

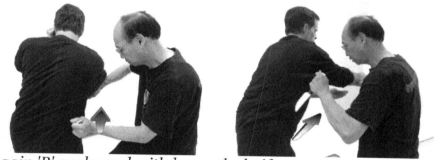

Again 'B' grabs and withdraws the knife

This time he still has a hold of the right wrist and reaching under the arm stabs to the midsection.

Scenario 4

Scenario 4) *When Player 'A' throws a right hook, Player 'B' blocks by driving his elbow into the biceps and*

Hacks (strikes) to the neck using the forearm and continues pushing down on the neck as he lifts the arm up in order to drive 'A's face into Player 'B's knee strike

Continuing with this clockwise motion he executes a head spin while still keeping control of the right arm

Grabbing the knife from the attacker and inserting it into the rib cage.

Notes

Chapter 10 - Ground Work

Fighting on the ground with a weapon is never a good idea. Why? Once you hit the ground with a weapon involved, your options are limited, your maneuverability is restricted and the chances of you getting injured or killed are greatly increased.

Because of the popularity of MMA many people have some knowledge of the art, either from TV or from actually taking a few classes. It is said that 90% of fights end up on the ground so like it or not you need some knowledge of what to do in case this happens to you, but it should not be your 'go to" technique.

The majority of assaults are rarely one on one; it is nearly always multiple attackers against one victim, which makes being on the ground even more dangerous. The important thing to remember is not to stay on the ground. Even if you are on top and winning you can bet that one of his friends will step in with a punch, kick or knife.

If you are taken to the ground get up as quickly as you can. If you can't immediately get to your feet, then maneuver to your back so that you can see what is coming your way and are able to defend against it. Don't roll over on your stomach or you are an easy target for a rear choke, knife in the back or stomp to the head. Remember: this is not a sport. You are not trying to get him to tap out, you are trying to survive.

Now that doesn't mean that you can't use locks and chokes, but you need to be more vicious with them. In the Southeast Asian arts you don't just apply a lock to get a submission you apply a lock and then break the joint or tear connective tissue so that the limb is useless.

It is important to understand the difference between sport and combat fighting and the difference between fighting barehanded and fighting against an opponent with a weapon. While you are trying to get him to tap out he can quickly grab his blade and start slicing and dicing on your leg or any part of your body that is near to his weapon.

Even if you don't see a weapon, don't assume that there is not one around. The assailant could have a knife in his pocket, hanging around his neck, his buddy could hand him one or he may have a 'push knife' hidden on his person.

Push knives are very small and easy to conceal, the blades are about 1"-2" inches long. They can be hidden in the waistband, jacket or even in the boot or shoe. There are push knives that can be interwoven into the shoelaces of your shoe to be used as an emergency weapon.

Push Knife

If you hit the ground all is not lost, keep him at a distance if you can by using your legs to kick the shins while you try to get back to your feet. Sometimes you can use being on the ground to your advantage if you have basic ground skills you may be able to pin the weapon between the ground and your hand while grabbing his arm, but this is only a temporary reprieve as he can easily switch the weapon to the other hand so you need to incapacitate him quickly.

Hopefully, you will never find yourself in this position, but it is a good idea to practice these scenarios just in case.

Ground 1

Ground 1) Player 'A' has fallen or been pushed to the ground, Player 'B' quickly moves in the take advantage of the situation

Note how Player 'A' lifts his shin into 'B's midsection to help to keep him at bay. You can also put your foot on his thigh if you cannot get your shin in place

With your left hand gripping his wrist, you will twist to apply pressure, (this is the same as the second angle #8 drill but now you are doing it while on the ground which will make it feel a whole lot different) grab the 'gatekeeper' with the right hand to continue the pressure to the wrist and disarm the knife

Finish with a cut to the throat

Ground 2

Ground 2) *As the attacker drives the knife forward you grab and twist to the right to move your body out of the way and to off balance him*

Notice the knee placement, this gives you room to maneuver

 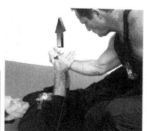 

Using the web of your hand you strip the knife straight up and into his neck

Ground 3

Ground 3) *Same situation, you grab and twist your body away from the attack*

But this time your foot is on his thigh, push your leg forward as hard as you can

This will drive his leg back and cause him to lose his balance, quickly roll up onto his arm

Disarm the knife and finish the attack.

Ground 4

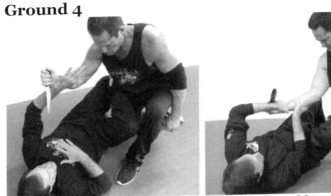

Ground 4) *Again Player 'A' finds himself on the ground, as Player 'B' strikes, 'A' moves his leg into position while grabbing the knife hand with both hands (notice the up and down grip)*

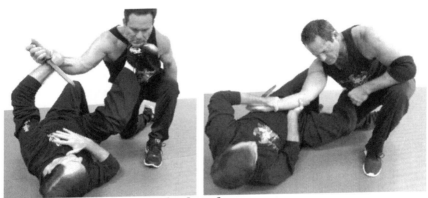

From here 'A' kicks to the head

Continues with the disarm and finishes

Ground 5

Ground 5) *Player 'A' attempts to drive the knife into Player 'B's chest*

Player 'B' blocks, grabs and twists the arm

From here 'B' pulls with his left arm and pushes with his right arm. This should cause 'A' to fall over his leg, from here 'B' will quickly disarm and counter.
Note: this actually works best for bigger guys, you could also try an arm drag with your right arm

Ground 6

Ground 6) *Now if you are smaller than your attacker you may want to try this variation:*
After you block, grab and twist the arm

Get your foot inside and place it on the chest using it to push him off and away from you

If you already have a good grip on the knife it should disarm as you push him back, quickly roll up into position and counter attack.

Click on or go to the link below to view the videos of the Drills and Techniques shown in this book and see how they are done.

http://bit.ly/2mFZPJJ

Notes

Final Thoughts

When looking for a self-defense school, course, book, or video make sure that it is street oriented and not for sport. You need to find something that is focused on protection for you and your family not scoring points or winning trophies.

Videos and books are great, but there is nothing like having a qualified instructor to explain to you the finer aspects of the techniques.

If you are serious about your training, then it is imperative that you practice. Just watching a video or reading a book is not enough. Don't get me wrong, it will help, but you need constant re-enforcement to keep your skills sharp.

Just like sports or any skill that you were good at when you were younger, but haven't participated in for years. You can't suddenly go out and play with the same skill and intensity as you did back then. Ask any weekend warrior.

Training with a partner can help to re-enforce confidence in your abilities. If you only practice a few times or practice in the air by yourself, you are never quite sure if you will be able to 'pull it off' when the need arises.

Working with a partner allows you to actually see that it works and provides you with the opportunity to make adjustments to the technique in order to make it your own.

I know that we are all busy, but it is a matter of priorities. I'm busy too, but if I used that for an excuse you would not be reading this book right now. You have to decide what activity is the most important to you.

As I have stated throughout the book avoidance of violence is always best, but sometimes it comes to you and should this happen you need to be ready for it.

Good luck with your training.

Appendices

To view video clips of some of the drills and techniques found in this book go to:

http://bit.ly/2mFZPJJ

Thanks for purchasing *"Secrets of the Knife" - Vol. 1*, and I hope that you have enjoyed it.

As an Independent author I don't have a big marketing department or the exposure of being on bookshelves in the mall.

If you enjoyed this book please help spread the work by telling your friends and leaving me a review on Amazon. Reviews are what helps the book to get noticed. The more reviews that I have the more it will help to get acknowledged in the search engines.

I appreciate your support by the purchase of this book. You are making it possible for me to continue to produce many more products such as this.

David Seiwert

Other books by the author:

*"**KunTao** - The esoteric martial art of Southeast Asia"*

*"Secrets of the **Karambit**"*

Available at our website or on Amazon

http://amzn.to/2mXsgEE

http://dfamediaproductions.com/books.html

Watch for "Secrets of the Knife - Volume 2" coming soon
This book will deal with Knife vs. Knife

Additional Reading

Secrets of the Karambit - David Seiwert

Way of the Raven Blade Combatives vol. 1 - Fernan Vargas

Knife Fighting: A Practical Course - Michael Janich

Balisong: The Lethal Art of Filipino Knife Fighting
 Gary Cagaanan & Sid Campbell

The Defensive Edge - Ron Balicki

Filipino Martial Culture - Mark Wiley

The Malay Art of Self-Defense - Sheikh Shamsuddin

 The Weapons & Fighting Arts of Indonesia - Donn F. Draeger

References

https://en.wikipedia.org/wiki/Clip_point

https://gearjunkie.com/knife-types-common-outdoors-blades

https://www.theknifeconnection.net/learn-about-knives/blade-types/

https://www.knife-depot.com/knife-information-112.html

https://www.knife-depot.com/knife-information-105.html

https://en.wikipedia.org/wiki/Clip_point

https://en.wikipedia.org/wiki/Macedonia_(ancient_kingdom)

https://en.wikipedia.org/wiki/Drop_point

https://www.knife-depot.com/tanto-knives/

http://www.knifeup.com/advantages-of-a-tanto-blade/

http://beebeknives.com/html/knife_anatomy.html

http://www.instructables.com/id/Lessons-of-a-Knife-making-the-ultimate-bush-tool/step3/Half-tang-vs-full-tang-Wood-vs-micarta/

http://www.survivalistboards.com/showthread.php?t=260928

https://lansky.com/index.php/blog/anatomy-knife-fixed-blade-knives-part-1-blade/#.V7EV8PdrhQI

https://en.wikipedia.org/wiki/Neolithic

http://www.bradshawfoundation.com/origins/oldowan_stone_tools.php

https://en.wikipedia.org/wiki/Chopper_(archaeology)

http://survivalist101.com/tutorials/survival-knives-101/parts-of-a-knife/

https://en.wikipedia.org/wiki/Knife

http://donscycleware.com/coteforknpa.html

http://www.cookingforengineers.com/article/130/Knife-Parts

https://lansky.com/index.php/blog/knife-blade-profiles-and-uses#.V_Bb0F6qNQJ

http://www.knifeup.com/all-the-types-of-knives-ever-made/

http://www.alloutdoor.com/2014/05/16/fixed-blade-edc/

http://www.hunterblades.com/fixed-blade-vs-folding-blade/

https://www.kabar.com/knives/detail/79

http://www.policemag.com/channel/patrol/articles/2009/06/weapon-retention-on-the-ground.aspx

http://www.military.com/military-fitness/close-quarters-combat/secret-to-surviving-ground-fight

http://modernsurvivalonline.com/fixed-blade-or-folding-survival-knives-which-is-better/

http://www.artofmanliness.com/2011/11/29/how-to-choose-the-perfect-survival-knife/

http://www.ltspecpro.com/Product/43LS/URBAN_PAL.aspx

https://www.kabar.com/knives/detail/79

https://malaymartialarts-silat.blogspot.com/2011/10/weapons-of-silat-in-malaysia.html

https://lansky.com/index.php/blog/knife-blade-profiles-and-uses#.V_Bb0F6qNQJ

https://en.wikipedia.org/wiki/Filipino_martial_arts

Notes

About the Author

 David Seiwert has been studying, teaching and training in a wide range of martial arts from Japan, Korea, China, Thailand, Indonesia and the Philippines since he was 12 years old.

He is recently retired from the engineering field and regularly travels to Southeast Asia to further increase his knowledge and understanding of these indigenous arts.

When not traveling he spends his time teaching, giving seminars, writing books and producing videos about the fighting systems of these regions.

For more information or training material on the martial arts, Mr. Seiwert can be contacted at:

www.DavidSeiwert.com
www.DynamicFightingArt.com
www.DfaMediaProductions.com

www.**DavidSeiwert.com**

www.**DynamicFightingArt.com**

www.**DfaMediaProductions.com**

questions@dynamicfightingart.com

Other books by the author:

"**KunTao** - The esoteric martial art of Southeast Asia"

"Secrets of the **Karambit**"

You can find more books and videos at our website
http://dfamediaproductions.com

Watch for "Secrets of the Knife - Volume 2" coming soon
This book will deal with Knife vs. Knife

Made in United States
Orlando, FL
02 March 2023

30589051R00115